When Mary was a girl
in Pennsylvania,
she knew she'd be
an artist one day.

In 1860, proper girls weren't artists.
They had polite hobbies—
flower arranging, needlepoint.
Not Mary.

Mary grew up tall
and temperamental,
the map of her fate
etched in her mind.
Just before her sixteenth birthday,
she charged down Chestnut Street,
raring to enroll in art school.
Mary was first on the list.

Mary studied hard at the Academy
and planned her next move.
She had to travel abroad.
A treasure trove of art
awaited her in Paris.
Her father grumbled.
Out of the question!
Mary held her course.

The Louvre Museum
was Mary's classroom.
She copied the Old Masters
and dreamed of seeing her art
in the celebrated show, the Salon.
Impossible!
Not for Mary.

Mary pressed her nose
against a gallery window,
absorbing pastel drawings
by Edgar Degas.
A riot of color!
She smiled and later said,
"I saw art then
as I wanted to see it."

Mary swept jewel tones
across her canvas.
She rendered cropped angles,
sparkling light.

The Salon judges
found her new work hasty,
her palette harsh.
Bah! What did they know?

The great Degas rapped
on Mary's studio door.
Join our band of independents,
he proposed.

We paint as we please.
We break the judges' rules.
Mary beamed.
"I began to live," she said.

Mary painted what she saw.
She captured
glimpses of life.
Her long hands flew,
dabbing brilliant tones,
lightning bolts of white.

Mary attended shows
at the theater,
her sketchbook in hand.

She strolled through museums,
her sister by her side.

Mary's outspoken opinions
echoed down aisles
lined with exotic Asian art.

Mary's family
came to live with her in Paris.
She painted her mother, her sister,
reading, sewing, drinking tea.
Her father might have been
a better model
if only he'd stayed awake!

Color splashed
across Mary's canvas—
canary yellow, radiant pink,
vibrant blue.
Pastel strokes flurried
over paper—
sharp and blurry,
straight and zigzagged.

Mary produced
a multitude of prints—
etchings, monotypes—
working with Degas
and on her own.
For Mary,
art was life.
Life was art.

Mary celebrated mothers
and their babies
in her paintings.
She sought and found truth.

Now her art
hangs in fine museums.
She proved that women
can be great artists, too.

MARY CASSATT was born in Allegheny City, Pennsylvania, in 1844. When she was seven years old, her family moved to Paris for two years. She learned to speak French and was probably influenced by great works of art throughout the city. A month before her sixteenth birthday, she signed up at the Pennsylvania Academy of the Fine Arts. She was the first in her class to enroll.

Mary was twenty-one years old when she decided to return to Paris. At that time, women were not admitted to the famous art school, the École des Beaux-Arts. Instead, she spent as much time as she could copying the Old Masters at the Louvre Museum and took private art lessons. She traveled throughout rural France and Spain, painting villagers in scenes of daily life. She studied church ceilings filled with angelic children in Italy.

One day she saw a display in a Paris gallery window of pastel works by Edgar Degas. Overwhelmed by their beauty, she returned again and again to study them. She said that seeing his work was "the turning point of my artistic life."

Degas saw Mary's paintings for the first time at the prestigious annual art exhibit, the Paris Salon of 1874. "She has infinite talent," he said. He had already joined a group of independent painters who snubbed the traditional Salon. That group later became known worldwide as the Impressionists and included Claude Monet, Pierre-Auguste Renoir, Paul Cézanne, Camille Pissarro, Alfred Sisley, and Berthe Morisot in its ranks. They had a fresh style featuring dabs of bright color and a spontaneous, sketch-like quality.

The Salon exhibited Mary's paintings several times, which was a huge accomplishment for an American woman. Then, in 1877, to her horror, both of her entries to the Salon were rejected. Degas invited her to join the independent painters. Mary combined forces with the group eagerly and exhibited with them for the first time in 1879. She never sent another painting to the Salon.

Mary's attachment to Degas was immediate. She had found someone whose opinionated attitude matched her own. Both artists were consumed with their work, their studios littered with canvases and paper in various stages of completion. Neither ever married.

While many of the artists in her independent group preferred landscapes, Mary was a figure painter. She rendered mothers and their babies, daughters, sisters, and grandmothers. Her family was a frequent subject of her work.

Although Mary treasured her friendship with Degas, she was wary of his fierce temper. "Sometimes it made him furious that he could not find a chink in my armor," she said. When she was commissioned to paint a mural for the Woman's Building at the World's Columbian Exposition in Chicago in 1893, Degas flew into a rage. How could she waste her time on "decorative art"? "I got my spirit up and said I would not give up the idea for anything," Mary said. She always followed her own path, a path that led to fame. She valued her independence.

Mary became a role model for generations of artists. She urged her American friends to buy Impressionist art and prompted its popularity in the United States. She believed in the power of art to inform, uplift, and inspire. By the time of her death in 1926 at the age of eighty-two, Mary was considered one of the best women painters of all time.

Her art can be seen in most major museums around the world.

Sources

Barter, Judith A., ed. *Mary Cassatt: Modern Woman*. Chicago: The Art Institute of Chicago, 1998.

Getlein, Frank. *Mary Cassatt: Paintings and Prints*. New York: Abbeville Press, 1980.

Harris, Lois V. *Mary Cassatt: Impressionist Painter*. Gretna, LA: Pelican Publishing Company, 2007.

Hyde, Margaret E. *Cassatt for Kids*. Santa Monica, CA: Budding Artists, Inc., 1996.

Mathews, Nancy Mowll, ed. *Cassatt and Her Circle: Selected Letters*. New York: Abbeville Press, 1984.

Mathews, Nancy Mowll. *Mary Cassatt: A Life*. New York: Villard Books, 1994.

Pollock, Griselda. *Mary Cassatt: Painter of Modern Women*. London: Thames & Hudson, 1998.

Sweeney, Joan, and Jennifer Heyd Wharton, illustrator. *Suzette and the Puppy: A Story About Mary Cassatt*. Hauppauge, NY: Barron's Educational Series, Inc., 2000.

Sweet, Frederick A. *Miss Mary Cassatt: Impressionist from Pennsylvania*. Norman, OK: University of Oklahoma Press, 1966.

Turner, Robyn Montana. *Portraits of Women Artists for Children: Mary Cassatt*. Boston: Little, Brown & Co., 1992.

Venezia, Mike. *Getting to Know the World's Greatest Artists: Mary Cassatt*. Chicago: Children's Press, 1993.

Webster, Sally. *Eve's Daughter/Modern Woman: A Mural by Mary Cassatt*. Chicago: University of Illinois Press, 2004.